EXPLORE
THE
U.S.A.

KENTUCKY

Anita Yasuda

LET'S READ AV² BY WEIGL™
ADDED VALUE • AUDIO VISUAL

Go to **www.av2books.com**, and enter this book's unique code.

BOOK CODE

V893059

AV² by Weigl brings you media enhanced books that support active learning.

AV² provides enriched content that supplements and complements this book. Weigl's AV² books strive to create inspired learning and engage young minds in a total learning experience.

Your AV² Media Enhanced books come alive with...

 Audio
Listen to sections of the book read aloud.

 Key Words
Study vocabulary, and complete a matching word activity.

 Video
Watch informative video clips.

 Quizzes
Test your knowledge.

 Embedded Weblinks
Gain additional information for research.

 Slide Show
View images and captions, and prepare a presentation.

 Try This!
Complete activities and hands-on experiments.

... and much, much more!

Published by AV² by Weigl
350 5th Avenue, 59th Floor
New York, NY 10118
Website: www.av2books.com   www.weigl.com

Library of Congress Cataloging-in-Publication Data
Yasuda, Anita.
 Kentucky / Anita Yasuda.
    p. cm. -- (Explore the U.S.A.)
Includes bibliographical references and index.
ISBN 978-1-61913-353-2 (hard cover : alk. paper)
1. Kentucky--Juvenile literature. I. Title.
F451.3.Y37 2012
976.9--dc23
                          2012015073

Printed in the United States of America in North Mankato, Minnesota
1 2 3 4 5 6 7 8 9 16 15 14 13 12

052012
WEP040512

Project Coordinator: Karen Durrie
Art Director: Terry Paulhus

Weigl acknowledges Getty Images as the primary image supplier for this title.

KENTUCKY

Contents

This is Kentucky.
It is called the Bluegrass State.
Bluegrass grows in Kentucky.

5

This is the shape of Kentucky.
It is in the south part
of the United States.
The Mississippi River flows
through Kentucky.

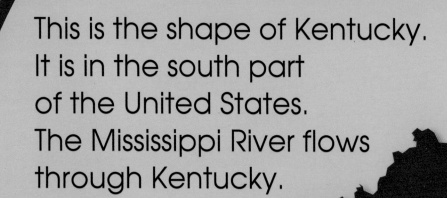

Where is Kentucky?

N
W E
S

Canada

United States

Pacific
Ocean

Atlantic
Ocean

Mexico

Kentucky borders
seven states.

Daniel Boone was a pioneer. He helped build a road from Virginia to Kentucky. Many settlers came to Kentucky on the road.

Daniel Boone helped the settlers build a fort.

Fort Boonesborough State Park

9

The goldenrod is the Kentucky state flower. Goldenrods grow to about 4 feet tall.

The state seal shows two men shaking hands.

The two men stand for friendship.

This is the state flag of Kentucky. It has the state seal and the state flower.

The Kentucky flag has words from a song.

CARROLL COUNTY
COURTHOUSE

13

The state bird of Kentucky is the cardinal. Cardinals sing about nine different songs.

Male cardinals have black masks.

This is the city of Frankfort. It is the capital city of Kentucky. Frankfort is one of the smallest capital cities in the country.

Four different buildings have been used for the Frankfort capitol since 1792.

Horses are raised in Kentucky. Kentucky has more than 320,000 horses.

Kentucky has a well known horse race called the Kentucky Derby.

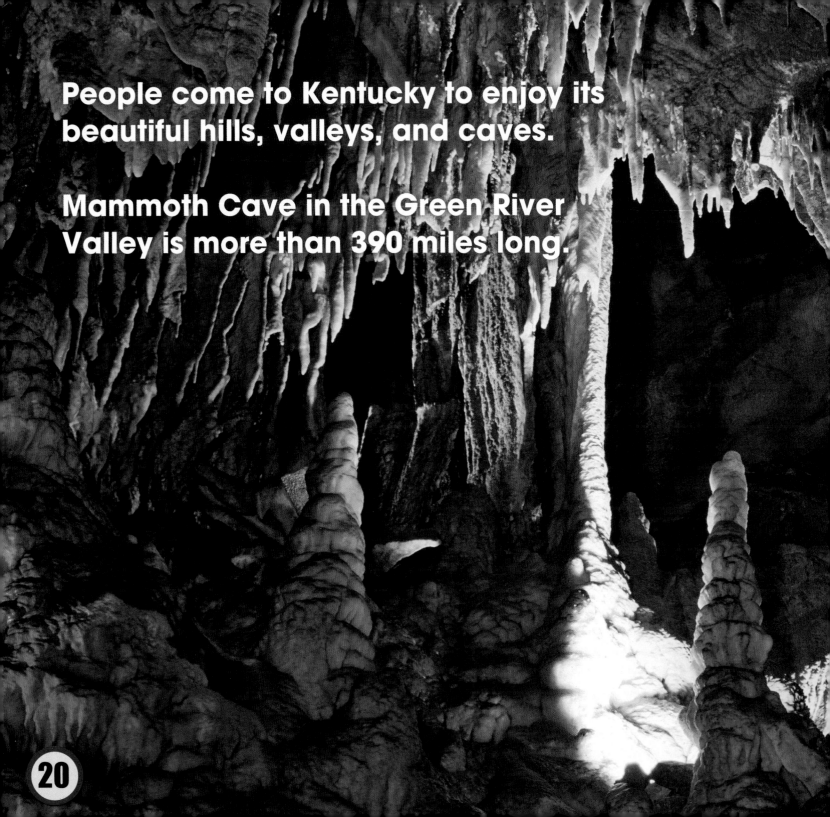

People come to Kentucky to enjoy its beautiful hills, valleys, and caves.

Mammoth Cave in the Green River Valley is more than 390 miles long.

KENTUCKY FACTS

These pages provide detailed information that expands on the interesting facts found in the book. These pages are intended to be used by adults as a learning support to help young readers round out their knowledge of each state in the *Explore the U.S.A.* series.

Pages 4–5

Kentucky bluegrass grows abundantly throughout the state. Bluegrass is named after the blue flowers that grow on the grass when the plant grows to its natural length. When not mown, bluegrass can reach a height of 2 to 3 feet (0.6 to 0.9 meters). Kentucky's Bluegrass region is a center for Thoroughbred horse breeding.

Pages 6–7

On June 1, 1792, Kentucky became the 15th state to join the United States. It lies in the south-central section of the United States. Ohio, Indiana, Illinois, West Virginia, Missouri, Virginia, and Tennessee border Kentucky. The northern border of Kentucky is formed by the Ohio River. Many early settlers came to Kentucky on the Ohio River.

Pages 8–9

Daniel Boone was a frontiersman and hero who helped blaze a trail and build a road known as the Wilderness Trail. It was an important route that led settlers through the Cumberland Gap into the Kentucky area. In 1775, Daniel Boone and a group of settlers established Fort Boonesborough. Many other settlements were soon created in Kentucky.

Pages 10–11

Goldenrod flowers have small bunches of golden blooms. Inventor Thomas Edison made rubber using goldenrod plants. Kentucky's state seal shows one man in buckskin and one man in formal dress shaking hands. The men represent the friendship between frontiersmen and statesmen, and their bond to protect national unity.

Pages 12–13

Kentucky's state flag has changed several times since the state joined the Union. The current flag was designed in the 1920s by an art teacher named Jessie Cox. The state motto, "United we stand, divided we fall," comes from The Liberty Song, a ballad written in 1768.

Pages 14–15

Cardinals build nests in the spring. They use small twigs, grasses, vines, and other plant materials. The female cardinal lays two to five eggs. She keeps the eggs warm while the male cardinal protects the nest.

Pages 16–17

Frankfort became the state capital of Kentucky in 1792. Frankfort has a population of about 28,000 people, making it the fifth-smallest state capital. Frankfort has many historic buildings, including the state capitol building, which combines Greek and French architectural styles.

Pages 18–19

Kentucky leads all states in the breeding of Thoroughbred horses. Thoroughbreds are the fastest horses in the world, reaching speeds of up to 45 miles (72 kilometers) per hour. Thoroughbred breeding earns $1.5 billion per year in Kentucky. Some of these horses compete in horse races at Churchill Downs racetrack in Louisville.

Pages 20–21

Mammoth Cave began to form about 10 million years ago. It is the longest known cave system in the world, with many underground rivers. Many rock formations are found in the cave. It was discovered in 1816 and has been open to tourists since. About 500,000 people tour the cave each year.

KEY WORDS

Research has shown that as much as 65 percent of all written material published in English is made up of 300 words. These 300 words cannot be taught using pictures or learned by sounding them out. They must be recognized by sight. This book contains 47 common sight words to help young readers improve their reading fluency and comprehension. This book also teaches young readers several important content words, such as proper nouns. These words are paired with pictures to aid in learning and improve understanding.

Page	Sight Words First Appearance
4	grows, in, is, it, state, the, this
7	of, part, through, where
8	a, came, from, he, many, on, was
11	about, feet, for, hands, men, shows, to, two
12	and, has, song, words
15	different, have
16	been, city, country, four, one, used
19	are, more, than, well
20	come, its, long, miles, people

Page	Content Words First Appearance
4	bluegrass, Kentucky
7	Mississippi River, shape, United States
8	Daniel Boone, fort, pioneer, road, settlers, Virginia
11	flower, friendship, goldenrod, seal
12	flag
15	bird, cardinal, masks
16	buildings, capitol, Frankfort
19	horses, Kentucky Derby, race
20	caves, Green River Valley, hills, Mammoth Cave, valleys

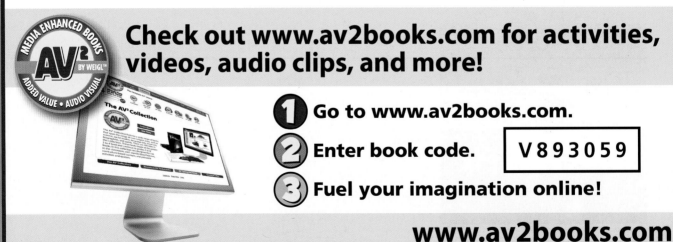